Moments

Grace Williams

BookLeaf
Publishing

India | USA | UK

Presentation by *BookLeaf Publishing*

Web: www.bookleafpub.com

E-mail: info@bookleafpub.com

ISBN: 9789357446266

First edition 2022

ACKNOWLEDGE MENT

To Mum and Dad Tom and Katie: To be perfectly honest I'm not sure why I'm dedicating this book to you - I did all the work! All you guys did was provide endless love, support, patience, guidance and encouragement and I guess I love you all and stuff.

To all my amazing friends: Okay listen here you lot - you have NO right being as incredibly kind, funny, compassionate, talented and amazing as you all are. Sort it out.

To my Grandparents, Aunts, Uncles and Cousins: Thank you guys for constantly bringing a smile to my face and believing in me, I don't know where I'd be without you. Possibly a smidge less awesome, if that's possible to believe.

And finally to Dylan, Jemima, Sherlock and Watson: I know you can't read this because you're all animals but that's your problem, not mine so I'm including you guys here anyway.

PREFACE

"It will all make sense again"
- Dodie Clark, Secret for the mad

Pepper's ghost

A trick of the light- that's all it takes.
A dancing pepper's ghost of a memory.
A moment reflected in rose tint.
A smell, A film, A song.

Who says time travel isn't real?

A good book

It's quiet here,
Peaceful.
Here, the given information
(And a little imagination)
Can help shape reality
Into whatever I need it to be.

When I'm here,
I can let go.
Time slips away,
And for a moment, I feel okay
Just sitting here, enjoying it all.

The people in the paragraphs
Can seem so real and alive.
Sometimes they'll stick with me,
Forever in my memory.

My favourite thing about these worlds
Is that they help me
temporarily forget my own.

I know that the outside world exists.

I know that I can't stay here for long.

So I'll enjoy this while it lasts.

Today I am angry

I left my house in a skirt today,
Without my tights.
I should've been able to do that
And feel safe
But I didn't.

I was running late and took a shortcut,
A quiet path away from the main road.
I should've been able to do that
And feel safe
But I didn't.

I wanted to go on a walk along the seafront
To clear my head, but it was dark.
I should've been able to do that
And feel safe
But I didn't.

I don't want to
tell my friends where I am if I'm out late.
I don't want to
keep my keys to hand.
I don't want to
keep looking over my shoulder.

I don't want to have to
take a different route
or stick to busy areas
or pretend to dawdle
or fake a phone call.

I want to feel safe.

It will be okay

It really will be okay
It doesn't sound it
Believe me- I know!
But it's true.

There will be a time
When a good cup of coffee,
A great movie,
Comfy socks,
Laughing at a joke,
Or the sun hitting a leaf

Will make you feel
Just that little bit more
Okay.

Tell me a story

Tell me the story
Of me
Tell me the story
Of you
Tell me the story
Of us
Tell me
Please.

I'd like to know.

One new message

The light of the screen hits my face,
Wincing slightly, I read the message.
It's late, and I really should be asleep,
But I open the phone anyway.

I can barely type through my blurry eyes,
Stinging under the light,
Weighed down by the long day.
Before I know it I'm hooked.

I feel wide awake,
and suddenly It's three hours later.
The thought of my alarm makes me wince,
But seeing as I'm up…

Maybe I should check that notification.
Maybe I should look at my to-do list.
Maybe I should delete that one thing.

Surely that can't hurt?

Three hours and a chat with my friend-
who also can't sleep- later:
I try again.

I make my apologies to my future self,
Turn the phone off,
Put it to one side,
And close my eyes.

Bzzzz

… maybe five more minutes.

Teacup

The teacup rattles
On the edge of the table.
If it falls it will break,
No matter how many times
The floor apologises.
But the question is
Can it be fixed?

Tongue-tied

It's there-
Right there!
On the tip of my tongue.

The answer
To the very simple question,
That I don't know why
I can't answer.

Close my eyes,
Take a deep breath,
And still nothing.

The words
Are simply
Nowhere
To be found.

I hope you can tell,
Though I'm not sure you can,
What I'm trying to say.

And by now,
The silence has gone on

Too long to go unnoticed.

Here we go again.

Photograph

An image forever trapped in time.
Their faces cheek to cheek,
Smiling and grinning
without a care in the world.

Before long though,
It will hurt to look at the photo,
But not long after that though,
It will stop hurting as much.

It will be changed
Beyond recognition,
Both the image and the memory,
Altered by arguments and apologies.

The photo will go on to hold
A lot of power
For such a small thing,
But right now none of that matters.

Right now, all it symbolises
Is an impromptu photoshoot
Taken hurridly, for a laugh,
Before heading out the door

Three two one... cheese!

I bet

I bet you couldn't wait to tell me.
I bet you thought you were being clever.
I bet you were secretly hoping I'd find out.
I bet you don't actually care what I think at all.
I bet you would do it again given the chance.
I bet you have torn yourself up about this.

And you won't ever do this again?

Yeah, I bet.

I'm alright

Missed the train,
But I'm alright.
Forgot my water bottle,
But I'm alright.
Dropped my phone,
But I'm alright.

Burnt dinner,
But I'm alright.
Tripped over on the pavement,
But I'm alright.
Forgot to get a present for a friend,
But I'm alright.

Spilt my drink on my favourite jeans,
But I'm alright.
Haven't handed in my assignment,
But I'm alright
My umbrella broke in the rain,
But I'm alright

"Are you alright?"
And suddenly,
No.
I'm not alright.

Not that I care

Not that I care but-
Kinda stung y'know,
When you had to leave.

It wasn't exactly
My favourite bit
Of news to receive.

You packed up your bags,
Music for the road,
And then off you went.

I picked myself up,
Looked out the window,
Closed the door and thought

This is it I guess.
So long, au revoir,
Good luck and all that.

.

Did you know how short you are?

Did you know how short you are?
Because I want to make sure you know!

Don't you think it would be funny
If I took something of yours,
Held it above your head,
And watched you jump for it?

Oh stop looking so sour,
You don't mind it really!

You know what else would be great?
If I invaded your personal space
And leant my arm on your head
Just 'cause you're the right size.

You look so adorable when you're angry!
Not that I care why you're upset.

What if I patted you on the head
Or picked you up and moved you
Or talked to you as if you were a child?

I bet you'd love that, wouldn't you!

What? Why are you leaving?
I didn't do anything wrong?

It was just a joke.

#fake

Find the right lighting,
Research the best hashtags,
And add an even cuter filter.
We all know this is fake - right?

Judge the way the light hits,
The cringy cliché hashtags,
The obnoxiously cute filter.
We all know this is fake - right?

Damned if you do.
Damned if you don't.
Either snobbish and above it all,
Or vacuous and one dimensional.

You try and work it out.

An acrostic poem about friends

For a couple of years now
Regardless of what's happened that day
I've had something to look forward to
Each lunchtime and after school.
Never failing to amaze me or make me laugh,
Despite all that I know you've been through.
So, anyway, I think you guys are alright

Long time no see

Brush off the dust
And look what I've found
A rare gem
I thought I'd lost

Something small,
Tiny and pure
How could I have forgotten
After all this time

Do I leave this?
Take it with me?
Forget this?
Or hold it tight?

A Haiku about stars

Gazing at the stars
I'm left to hope and wonder
At all that has been

A poem about writing a poem

I need to write a poem,
But I can't think of anything.
I want something a little self-aware
I'm after something fun
Without being trite or twee

Done that idea
That idea is too difficult
Maybe *this* could work?..

Then it hits me
Like a jolt of electricity
And I rush to get my pen

It's cheesy, simple, fun,
A little tongue in cheek,
Absolutely perfect.

Soon the poem is finished,
My only hope is that
It was fun to read.

www.ingramcontent.com/pod-product-compliance
Lightning Source LLC
La Vergne TN
LVHW021350200726

843509LV00014B/2775

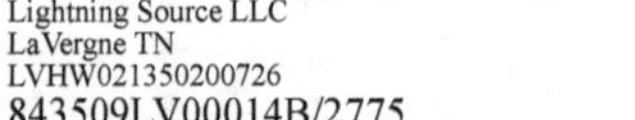